Victorian Life
Schools

D0188132

Nicola Barber

WAYLAND

First published in 2008 by Wayland

Copyright © Wayland 2008

Editor: Katie Powell
Designer: Jane Hawkins
Concept design: Paul Cherrill

Wayland
338 Euston Road
London NW1 3BH

Wayland Australia
Level 17/207 Kent Street
Sydney, NSW 2000

All rights reserved

British Library Cataloguing in Publication Data
 Barber, Nicola
   School. - (Victorian life)
   1. School children - Great Britain - History - 19th
   century - Juvenile literature 2. Schools - Great
   Britain - History - 19th century - Juvenile literature
   3. Great Britain - Social life and customs - 19th
   century - Juvenile literature
   I. Title
   371'.00941'09034
ISBN 978 0 7502 5369 7

Picture acknowledgements: Bettmann/Corbis: 24
brinkstock/Alamy: 20, Mary Evans Picture Library:
7, 8, 10, 12, 14, 15, 16, 19, 26, 27, Hulton Archive/Getty
Images: 21R, 2d Alan King/Alamy: 13 Museum of
Dartmoor Life: 18B, c.2004 TopFoto/TopFoto.co.uk:
Cover (Main Image), 9, Topham Picturepoint/
TopFoto.co.uk: 3, 22, Visual Arts Library (London): 11
Wayland Archive: Cover (BR), 4-5, 6, 17, 18T, 21L, 25,
28, 30, West Glamorgan Archive Service: 23

With thanks to Wrexham Heritage Services for the kind
reproduction of the extract on p17, to Powys County
Archives Office for the extract on p19, to Stretton
Handley Primary school for the extract on p23 and to
History House (www.historyhouse.co.uk) for the
extract on p25.

Printed in China

Wayland is a division of Hachette Children's Books,
an Hachette Livre UK company
www.hachettelivre.co.uk

BEDFORD BOROUGH LIBRARIES

939318003

13-Oct-2010

370.9

J 371.00 q Bar

Contents

Words in **bold** can be found in the glossary.

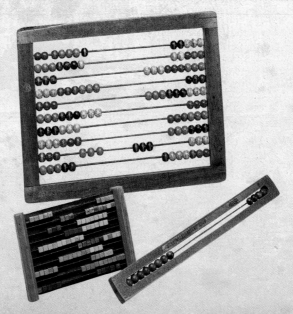

Victorian school life

Queen Victoria came to the throne in 1837 and **reigned** for 64 years until her death in 1901. These six decades were a time of huge change in Britain.

Changing times

The population of the country more than doubled during this time. The **Industrial Revolution** saw thousands of people moving from rural areas to towns and cities, and the development of the railways changed the way people lived and worked forever. There were huge advances in education, too. At the beginning of Queen Victoria's reign, very few children even attended school. By the time of her death school was both **compulsory** and free.

Milestones in education

Before 1833, most schools were run and funded by church societies. In 1833, the government became involved in education for the first time. It agreed to give £20,000 a year to these organisations to help them build schools.

This Sunday School educated poor children who could not afford to go to a regular school as they had to work during the week.

It was not until 1870 that the government passed its Elementary Education Act. This was intended to provide education for the many thousands of children who were not already attending a school. The schools set up under this act were run by a board of locally elected people, and were known as **Board Schools**.

Half-timers

By 1880, there were about 4,000 Board Schools, and school was made compulsory for the first time for children up to 10 years of age. School was not free however, and many poor families struggled to find even the smallest fees charged for their children's education. Some children, called 'half-timers', had to combine their schoolwork with paid work, as their families needed them to earn a wage. In 1891, the government finally gave grants to make education free in all **elementary schools**.

Written at the time

During Victoria's reign people began slowly to realise that educating both the rich and the poor was good for the country. In 1894, the writer Sir Arthur Conan Doyle sums up this view of the country's schools in his story, *The Naval Treaty* for the *Strand Magazine*:

'Lighthouses my boy! Beacons of the future! Capsules, with hundreds of bright little seeds in each, out of which will spring the wiser, better England of the future.'

⬆ Boys stand in neat rows for a music lesson at a Board School in 1895.

Who went to school?

In 1837, nearly half of all the children in Britain did not go to school. Many of those who did go barely learned to read or write. There was no national system of schools and it was not until 1833 that the government finally accepted responsibility for any involvement in education.

Income

Whether or not a child went to school depended largely on the income of his or her family. Wealthy parents could afford to send their sons to one of the large **public schools**, while their daughters were mostly educated at home. Middle-class children often went to small private schools in their local towns. However, poor children may not have attended school at all, mainly because their families needed them to earn money. Children as young as four or five were sent to work in mines, factories and mills. If they were lucky, these children might attend a church Sunday School where they would learn about the Bible.

Young children doing back-breaking work in a brickyard in 1871.

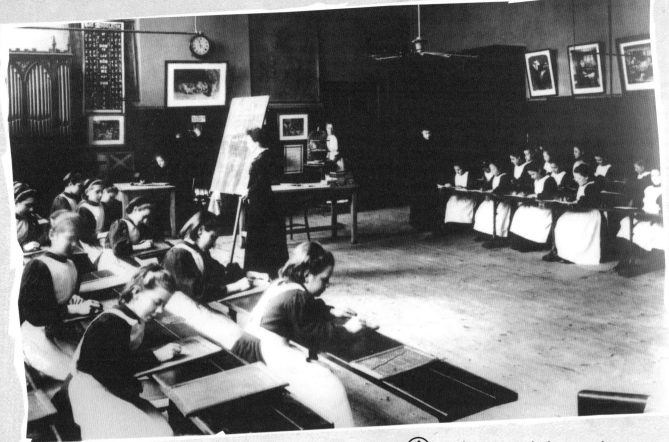

⬆ Girls sit in orderly rows for their lessons at St. Marylebone School in London in 1890.

Belief

In the early Victorian years, many people thought that the children of the working classes did not need to go to school. They believed that educating such children might make them unruly and difficult and would make them 'rise above their station'. But, reformers such as the Earl of Shaftesbury, William Forster and the writer Charles Dickens argued that education should be for all children.

Anthony Ashley Cooper, 1801–1885

Throughout his life, the 7th Earl of Shaftesbury, Anthony Ashley Cooper, used his position and influence to try to improve working conditions for the poor. In particular he produced several reports that revealed the grim conditions in the country's mines and factories. Many people were appalled to find that small children often spent up to eighteen hours in the dark, dragging heavy loads of coal. Lord Ashley's reports prompted parliament to pass several acts to regulate child labour. He was also interested in education for the poor, and was chairman of the Ragged Schools Union for nearly 40 years.

Schools for the poor

As the Victorian age progressed, people's opinions about education for the poor began to change. Many people realised that an educated population would help to make the country more **prosperous**.

Elementary Education Act 1870

This change in attitude was reflected by the increasing interest taken in education by the government. In 1870, the Elementary Education Act established schools for children between the ages of five and ten.

This Education Act did not make school either free or compulsory. Most Victorian schools charged fees which many poor people simply could not afford. Such families also couldn't afford to lose the income brought in by their children, so many poor children continued to go to work rather than attend school. For those who could afford it, the cheapest education was often at a **dame school**, so-called because such schools were often run by elderly ladies.

⬇ This engraving from the *Illustrated News of the World*, in 1858, shows a dame teacher teaching her pupils the alphabet.

⬆ A chaotic scene at a Ragged School in Smithfield, London, as depicted by the book illustrator George Cruikshank.

Ragged Schools

Children in **workhouses** attended classes in the mornings, and many churches and charities ran free schools for the poorest children. The most famous of these charities was the **Ragged Schools** Union which was established in 1844. The Ragged Schools provided free education for the very poorest, homeless children.

By 1870, there were more than 350 of these schools around the country. As well as giving children a basic education, the Ragged Schools often provided a place to eat and, in the winters, shelter from the cold.

Written at the time

In a letter to the *Daily News* in 1852, Charles Dickens describes the appearance of the children who attend Field Lane Ragged School in London:

'They who are too ragged, wretched, filthy, and forlorn, to enter any other place: who could gain admission into no charity-school, and who would be driven from any church-door: are invited to come in here, and find some people not depraved [wicked], willing to teach them something, and show them some sympathy ... '

Private education

Sons from wealthy families were often sent to **grammar schools** or **boarding schools**. Many of the boarding schools were expensive public schools that had been founded hundreds of years before Queen Victoria came to the throne.

⬆ Boys and their teacher at a small public school in London in 1900.

Life at public school

The education at Victorian public schools focused on the classics – Latin and Greek language and literature. Boys needed to study these subjects in order to go to university, or to enter a **profession**. Life could be tough in these schools – the younger boys were expected to run errands for the older boys, which was called 'fagging'. Sport was also considered to be very important, particularly team sports which were thought to be healthy for boys, and taught them to try their best while always playing by the rules.

Fact and fiction

Public schools were not funded by the government, and were therefore not checked or regulated. In some of the smaller boarding schools, conditions for the boys could be atrocious. Many of these schools were places for unwanted children who stayed there all year round. In 1838, the writer Charles Dickens travelled to Yorkshire to see for himself what conditions were like in such schools. In his novel, *Nicholas Nickleby* he described the pathetic condition of the boys in his fictional school, Dotheboys Hall as 'pale and haggard faces, lank and bony figures, children with the countenances of old men, deformities with irons upon their limbs, boys of stunted growth, and others whose long meagre legs would hardly bear their stooping bodies.'

⇧ Boys stand at the entrance to a playing field at Eton College, Berkshire. Public schools such as Eton and Rugby placed great emphasis on sport.

Thomas Arnold, 1795–1842

The most famous headmaster of Rugby School, Thomas Arnold, was responsible for many reforms at Rugby which had a huge influence on education in all public schools. He introduced subjects such as mathematics, history and modern languages into the curriculum. He considered learning to be just part of the more important aim of education – the formation of character. His aim was to train boys to be Christian 'gentlemen'. His methods were described in 1857 in 'Tom Brown's Schooldays', a novel by Thomas Hughes who was a pupil at Rugby when Arnold was headmaster.

13

Education for girls

In most wealthy families, girls were taught at home by **governesses**. Many Victorians considered it a waste of time to educate girls at school.

Family life

Most governesses were educated, middle-class ladies who were forced to work because of their financial situations. Governesses were not servants but neither were they part of the family. As well as reading, writing and arithmetic, they taught their pupils subjects that were considered essential for a woman's place in society, such as French, music and painting.

As a young girl, Queen Victoria was educated by a governess.

Board Schools

At the Board Schools established by the Education Act of 1870, boys and girls were often educated separately. As well as learning the basics of reading, writing and arithmetic, in some schools girls were taught **housewifery** – skills such as washing, ironing, cleaning and cooking.

Schools for girls

The Victorian age also saw the foundation of schools that aimed to give girls as good an education as boys. Reformers such as Dorothea Beale and Frances Buss (1827–1894) pioneered the improvement of girls' education, introducing academic subjects and campaigning for girls to be allowed to apply to university. Frances Buss founded the North London Collegiate School in 1850. It was a private, **fee-paying** school, but, in the 1870s, Buss turned it into a grammar school with no fees so that working class girls could also have a good education.

Dorothea Beale, (1831–1906)

Dorothea Beale was the headmistress of Cheltenham Ladies' College from 1858 until her death in 1906. She transformed the school by introducing academic subjects such as science, mathematics, French and Latin. She also founded St Hilda's, a college for girls at Oxford University.

The school day

The headteacher of a school was responsible
for drawing up the timetable for the school week.
Each day the children had a mixture of lessons,
as well as prayers and time to learn practical skills.

School hours

The school day began at around 9 o'clock and finished at about 4 o'clock.
At midday there was a long break for lunch, during which most children
went home. Some children lived too far away to walk home so they brought
their lunch with them. School started again at 2 o'clock and finished after
afternoon prayers.

Through the day

Mornings were usually
devoted to the 'three Rs,'
as well as Scripture. In
the afternoon there was
more variety. Depending
on what 'standard' they
were in, children might
have 'drill', singing,
dictation and recitation.

⇐ In this photograph,
boys are exercising in
their school grounds.

16

Written at the time

This extract is from the rules of a school in Rossett, North Wales, in 1859:

'11. The hours of school are from 9 to 12, and from 2 to 5 in Summer; and from 9 to 12, and from 2 to 4 in Winter.

12. Saturday will be a whole holiday. There will be one week's holiday at Christmas — one at Easter — and a month during the Harvest.

13. Every child will be expected to attend the Sunday School unless given permission otherwise prior to admission.'

During dictation the teacher read out a passage for the children to write out. Recitation involved learning a poem or passage of text off by heart to recite out loud.

Another type of lesson was the object lesson. In this lesson children examined an object such as a hairbrush, or wool, or a candle, while the teacher read out facts about it. In some schools boys learned practical skills such as woodwork, while girls did needlework or other housewifery skills. History and geography were taught, too, although they were not compulsory subjects.

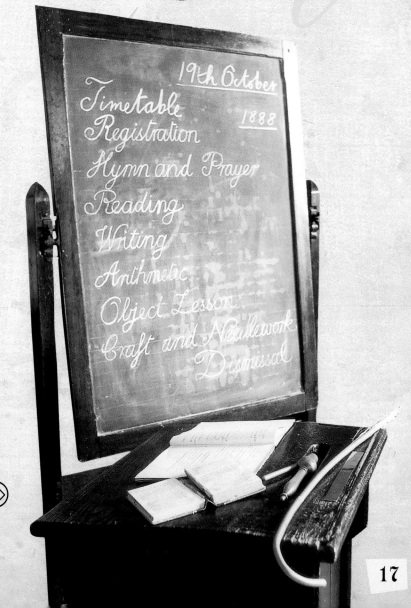

A timetable for a typical school day in 1888.

What did they learn?

Victorian children spent a lot of their time learning the 'three Rs': Reading, wRiting and aRithmetic. Children learned by copying and reciting letters and words, and they were all expected to learn at the same speed.

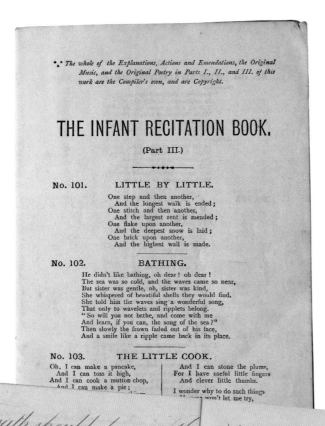

.•. *The whole of the Explanations, Actions and Emendations, the Original Music, and the Original Poetry in Parts I., II., and III. of this work are the Compiler's own, and are Copyright.*

THE INFANT RECITATION BOOK.
(Part III.)

No. 101.   LITTLE BY LITTLE.

One step and then another,
   And the longest walk is ended;
One stitch and then another,
   And the largest rent is mended;
One flake upon another,
   And the deepest snow is laid;
One brick upon another,
   And the highest wall is made.

No. 102.   BATHING.

He didn't like bathing, oh dear! oh dear!
The sea was so cold, and the waves came so near,
But sister was gentle, oh, sister was kind,
She whispered of beautiful shells they would find.
She told him the waves sing a wonderful song,
That only to wavelets and ripplets belong.
"So will you not bathe, and come with me
And learn, if you can, the song of the sea?"
Then slowly the frown faded out of his face,
And a smile like a ripple came back in its place.

No. 103.   THE LITTLE COOK.

Oh, I can make a pancake,
   And I can toss it high,
And I can cook a mutton chop,
   And I can make a pie;
And I can stone the plums,
For I have useful little fingers
   And clever little thumbs.
I wonder why to do such things
   They won't let me try,

Learning to read

Most schools had very few books, and in many schools the Bible was the main 'reader'. The children lined up in silence and waited their turn to read aloud from the Bible, often stumbling over the long, difficult words.

Standards

Children in Victorian schools were divided into six different 'standards'. Government inspectors visited schools regularly to test the children. If children failed the test they had to repeat the whole standard.

⬅ Children were expected to learn lines of poetry off by heart from books such as this 'Infant Recitation Book', and to practise their handwriting in copybooks.

18

Written at the time

This report was written in 1895 after government inspectors visited a small school in rural Wales. The inspectors were not impressed:

'This little school, I regret to have to report, is in a backward condition. The Reading in the first and second standards and the Spelling in the second standard were weak; the Arithmetic in the first standard was practically a failure: some of the children in it could not take the sums down, and others attempted to do the sums by means of strokes on their slates. Out of 19 examined in the whole school in Arithmetic only two passed well, seven just barely passed, and ten failed, and out of these ten, six had no sums right.'

This meant that there were often older children in the same class as much younger children. In 1862 a code was introduced which laid down exactly what children should know for each standard. In the same year, the government also introduced 'payment by results' for teachers. This meant that teachers' wages were cut if their pupils' results were poor. This system was very unfair as it penalised teachers who taught in the worst schools. It came to an end in 1897.

While geography was not a compulsory subject, it was still taught in many Victorian schools.

The schoolroom

In the early years of Queen Victoria's reign all sorts of buildings were used as schools. Public schools often had grand buildings, but schools for the poor were set up in church halls, in people's houses and even in barns.

⬆ Many Victorian buildings are still used as schools today.

New schools

After the 1870 Education Act, more new schools were built. Many of these schools followed the design set by an architect called E. R. Robson, who was employed by the London School Board from 1872 until 1889. Robson's plan for a typical school had a central assembly hall with classrooms off three sides. Windows were set high up in the walls to prevent children from being distracted during their lessons. In smaller rural places, schools often had just one large classroom for all of the children.

The Victorian classroom

In a classroom, boys and girls sat at desks in rows, facing the teacher. The teacher's desk was often on a raised platform so that he or she could see what was going on at the back of the room. The pupils' desks usually had lids with space inside for books, and shelves beneath, or a hook on the side, to store writing slates. Paper was expensive, so children learned to write on these slates, which could be cleaned and used over and over again. The teacher wrote with chalk on a blackboard at the front of the class. Many schools had an **abacus** to help the children learn maths.

A day in the life of...

...a Victorian teacher:

'My day starts at 7 in the morning when I wake and prepare for school. My small house is next door to the school, so I do not have far to go for the start of school at ten to nine. The children line up and enter the classroom in silence. I notice that there are several absences due to illness and because it is harvest time. I call out each name and the children answer with a bow or curtsey. Then they sit down. After morning prayers we start our lessons: Scripture, spelling, mathematics and poetry recitation. We end the morning with more prayers and then the children go home for lunch. School starts again at 2 o'clock with an inspection of hands and shoes for cleanliness. This afternoon is an object lesson. Sadly, I feel it is my duty to beat a child for unruly behaviour. Our school day ends at 4.30, and once the children are gone I settle down to write up the events of the week in the log book.'

Young children were taught to count using an abacus.

Children learned to write on slates such as this one.

Teachers

In poorer schools, the quality of teaching varied widely. In many church schools and Board Schools, one teacher could be in charge of a room full of 100 pupils or more. In these schools, the teacher was usually helped by older children, called monitors.

Teacher training

Teachers in boys' grammar and public schools had usually studied at university, but most did not have any special teacher training. Both Dorothea Beale and Frances Buss trained as teachers, and were proud of the fact that they only employed qualified teachers in their schools. They were amongst the earliest pupils at Queen's College for Ladies in London, which was founded in 1843 to train girls to be teachers.

Pupil-teachers

In 1846, a system of training pupil-teachers was established by the government. It meant that pupils who were aged 13 or above could train to be teachers at the same time as completing their own studies.

A Victorian school in the 1880s. The children took turns to do exercises in order to keep warm.

After five years of side-by-side training and education the pupil-teachers could then study for a teacher's certificate.

Log books

From 1862 onwards, head teachers had to keep **log books** to record what had happened in their schools week by week. Many of these log books survive today, and they provide a fascinating insight into life in Victorian schools. They also show the difficulties experienced by many Victorian teachers. School buildings were often cold, damp and poorly lit. Children who were unused to going to school could be unruly and rude and diseases, such as scarlet fever and or measles, could shut down a school for fear of the spread of infection.

School log books show the difficulties faced by many Victorian teachers.

Written at the time

These extracts are taken from the log book of Stretton Handley School in Derbyshire:

'It was impossible to go on with the proper lessons until about half past nine, as the school was full of smoke from the stoves, until we could not see across ...' (1890)

'The children did arithmetic this afternoon instead of needlework as it was too dark to do needlework ...' (1882)

'Richard Wilson threw a stone in coming to school this morning and killed a chicken ...' (1882)

Discipline

Discipline in Victorian schools was very strict. In general, most Victorians thought that it was wrong to be too kind towards children as it only encouraged bad behaviour. Children were expected to 'be seen but not heard'.

Punishments

Lessons often took place in silence, except when the teacher asked a question. Children were punished for bad behaviour or if they were late. They were also punished for untidy work, and for mistakes such as forgetting their times tables or spelling a word incorrectly. For such poor work, children were usually made to stand in front of their classmates wearing a dunce's cap – a hat with a D for dunce pinned onto it.

Teachers also used a short leather strap to punish offences such as talking, lying or being lazy, often with a few blows across the hand. For even more serious misbehaviour such as thieving, a cane was used to beat the offender.

A boy is made to wear a dunce's cap as a punishment at a school in 1867.

Written at the time

Entries in this school log book from the 1880s show the kind of offences that resulted in punishment, and highlight the problem of pupils not turning up for school:

18 June 1880: 'Two or three boys slightly punished this week for indolence and obstinacy ... '

16 July 1880: 'Many of the cottagers here have good gardens stocked with fruit trees, and the picking of gooseberries and currants, now ripe, accounts for the non-attendance of so many children whose nimble fingers are doing their parents good service.'

23 July 1880: 'Haying and fruit-picking still keep down attendance ... '

8 October 1880: 'Eliza Malyon, a girl, who has always given as much trouble as she dared give, was punished on Thursday for obstinacy and hindering the progress of a lesson.'

29 October 1880: 'Acorn picking is the cause of absence now.'

1 December 1882: 'William Jarvis flogged for insulting an old man, as soon as he left the school premises.'

Rewards

As well as punishments there was also a system of rewards in Victorian schools. Good work was given points or stars, and if a pupil had worked hard he or she might receive a certificate, or a prize such as a book, at the end of the year. There were also medals for children who did not miss school. Attendance remained a big problem until school was made free and compulsory in 1891. Poor parents could not afford the fees charged by schools, and in rural areas many children were kept out of school to work in the fields.

Medals and certificates were given for good work and regular school attendance.

Sport and recreation

Sport played an important part in school life. The Latin saying *mens sana in corpore sano* – 'a sound mind in a healthy body' was adopted by many public schools, where fresh air and exercise were considered vital for health.

Team games

Some public schools had their own games, for example 'fives' which was played by hitting a ball against the walls of an inside court with bare or gloved hands. Eton, Winchester, Rugby and Clifton all had their own different variations of this game. The game of rugby was invented at Rugby School in 1823 and cricket was also widely played.

⬆ The game of rugby as it was played at Rugby School in the early nineteenth century.

Written at the time

This extract comes from *Tom Brown's Schooldays* by Thomas Hughes, a pupil at Rugby school. It describes a dramatic moment in a rugby match played on the close in 1857:

'Then a moment's pause, while both sides look up at the spinning ball. There it flies, straight between the two posts, some five feet above the cross-bar, an unquestioned goal; and a shout of real, genuine joy rings out from the School-house players-up, and a faint echo of it comes over the close from the goal-keepers under the Doctor's wall. A goal in the first hour – such a thing hasn't been done in the School-house match these five years.'

Drill and playtime

At poorer schools, the pupils did not usually play team games, but from 1871 'drill' became part of the **curriculum**. For 'drill' the children stood in neat rows, usually outside on the playground, and lifted their arms or legs, or marched on the spot, all to commands given by the teacher. Drill was a good way to exercise lots of children at once, but it was probably not much fun for the pupils. They must have looked forward to playtime, which happened halfway through morning lessons. The children played with hoops or skipping ropes, or chalked hopscotch on the ground. Some had marbles, tiddlywinks or conkers, while boys sometimes used a blown-up pig's bladder as a football to kick around.

Girls playing *Ring O' Roses* in the school playground in 1850.

Timeline

1837   Queen Victoria comes to the throne.

1838–1839 Charles Dickens' novel, *Nicholas Nickleby* is published.

1842   Lord Ashley's (Earl of Shaftesbury) Coal Mines Act prohibits women and children from working underground.

1843   The Queen's College for Ladies is founded as a teacher traning college.

1844   The Ragged Schools Union is established.

1846   The system for training pupil-teachers is established.

1850   North London Collegiate School is founded by Frances Buss – a pioneer in education for girls.

1857   Thomas Hughes' novel, *Tom Brown's Schooldays* is published.

1858   Dorothea Beale becomes headmistress of Cheltenham Ladies' College.

1862   The Revised Code is established, introducing 'payment by results' for teachers.

1869   The first residential college for women, Girton College, is founded at Cambridge University.

1870   The Elementary Education Act establishes Board Schools for children between the ages of five and ten.

1880   Education becomes compulsory for children aged between five and ten years of age.

1891   The Elementary Education Act makes education free in all elementary schools.

1893   The Elementary Education Act raises the school leaving age from ten years of age to 11 years of age.

1897   The revised code for 'payment by results' is finally abolished.

1901   Queen Victoria dies.

Glossary

abacus a frame with beads that slide along rods to help with counting, addition and subraction

Board School schools run by a board of locally elected people, established by the Elementary Education Act of 1870. Local school boards were abolished in 1902

boarding school a school in which pupils live ('board') during term time

classics refers to the ancient classical civilizations of Greece and Rome, their language and literature

compulsory describes something that has to be done

curriculum describes all the subjects taught at a school

dame school an early type of school, often run by an elderly woman. The quality of education at such schools was highly variable

elementary school primary school

fee-paying a school that charges fees

governess a woman who teaches the children of a family, in their family home

grammar school a secondary school that offered a good education to children of all social classes

housewifery describes the jobs associated with running a home such as cooking, cleaning and tidying

income money received in return for work

Industrial Revolution the name given to a time when steam-powered machinery was developed to do jobs previously done by hand. The Industrial Revolution took place in Britain during the end of the eighteenth and beginning of the nineteenth centuries

log book a book that is used to keep a record of events

profession a paid job

prosperous successful and wealthy

public school a private school that charges fees

Ragged School in the Victorian period, a school for destitute children

reign the number of years a king or queen rules a country

standard the grades used in Victorian schools, which were tested by a government examiner

workhouse a place where the sick and destitute could seek shelter and food in return for work

Index

Resources

The History Detective Investigates: Victorian School Richard Wood, Wayland 2002

Victorian Childhood: At School Ruth Thomson, Franklin Watts 2007

You Wouldn't Want to Be a Victorian Schoolchild: Lessons You'd Rather Not Learn John Malam, Wayland 2002

www.bbc.co.uk/schools/victorians

An excellent website that summarises Victorian life.

www.victorianweb.org

Explore many different topics about the Victorians.